Farming in the 1800s

by Kathleen Cox

Editorial Offices: Glenview, Illinois • Parsippany, New Jersey • New York, New York
Sales Offices: Needham, Massachusetts • Duluth, Georgia • Glenview, Illinois
Coppell, Texas • Ontario, California • Mesa, Arizona

Photographs

Every effort has been made to secure permission and provide appropriate credit for photographic material. The publisher deeply regrets any omission and pledges to correct errors called to its attention in subsequent editions.

Unless otherwise acknowledged, all photographs are the property of Scott Foresman, a division of Pearson Education.

Photo locators denoted as follows: Top (T), Center (C), Bottom (B), Left (L), Right (R), Background (Bkgd).

Opener: Library of Congress; 3 Library of Congress; 4 (BL, CC) Library of Congress; 6 (BL) Museum of English Rural Life, University of Reading/©DK Images, (C) Nebraska State Historical Society; 8 (B) ©DK Images, (C) Library of Congress; 10 Library of Congress; 12 (BL) ©DK Images, (B) Library of Congress; 14 Library of Congress; 16 Library of Congress; 18 Library of Congress; 19 ©DK Images; 20 Denver Public Library/Western History Collection; 21 ©DK Images; 22 ©Museum of London/©DK Images; 23 Library of Congress

ISBN: 0-328-13613-1

Copyright © Pearson Education, Inc.

All Rights Reserved. Printed in the United States of America. This publication is protected by Copyright, and permission should be obtained from the publisher prior to any prohibited reproduction, storage in a retrieval system, or transmission in any form by any means, electronic, mechanical, photocopying, recording, or likewise. For information regarding permission(s), write to: Permissions Department, Scott Foresman, 1900 East Lake Avenue, Glenview, Illinois 60025.

7 8 9 10 V0G1 14 13 12 11 10 09 08

Farming As a Way of Life

During the 1800s, many people worked the land as farmers. Sometimes it was by choice; other times it was not. People with a small amount of money may have bought land to start an apple orchard. Those with little or no money farmed land they did not own. They were called sharecroppers, and they had to work to pay for using someone else's land. Enslaved people often were forced to work on plantations by plantation owners.

Farming became the main way to make money during this time period. It helped make the country wealthy because the crops were sold to other countries. By the middle of the century, the country's population was just more than 23 million. Half of all Americans farmed for a living. But farming was very challenging work.

Farming in the 1800s was hard work. Horse-drawn plows were used to cut through the soil.

Farm life demanded hard physical work seven days a week. One thing that made farming especially difficult was forces that farmers could not control. Their crops could be destroyed by plant diseases, insects, or by too much or too little rain.

Technology that is common today did not exist in the 1800s. Electricity wasn't a source of power until the late 1800s. Even **kerosene** lanterns weren't widely available until the 1860s. For many farming families these lanterns were too expensive. When working before sunrise and after sunset, most people relied on candles. They often made the candles themselves.

People who lived on farms and plantations drew water from a well or collected it from a nearby stream. Women and children then carried the water. They used two pails hung on the ends of a yoke, or pole, to carry the water on their shoulders.

Getting around wasn't easy in the 1800s either. Dirt roads or tracks linked most communities together. Railroad construction did not begin until 1830. Most people who lived on farms traveled by horse, horse and buggy, horse and wagon, or they walked. This often meant walking miles to visit a neighboring farm or town. Trips to the nearest market turned into important all-day journeys.

Farmers had to rely on the power of pack animals and their own strength to farm their land and produce their crops.

Tools for farming were often made of simple wood and iron. They were nothing like the machinery found on today's farms. Until the 1850s, farmers mostly used hand tools to prepare their fields and harvest their crops. They cleared their land with basic wood plows, which they slowly worked through the rough land to loosen the soil. They sowed seeds and pulled weeds by hand. Finally, they picked each individual piece of fruit or boll of cotton with their hands. They walked through their fields swinging a heavy sickle—a tool with a sharp curved blade—back and forth, cutting and harvesting grains.

Farmers in the 1800s relied on horses and their own strength to plow, plant, and harvest.

Work was exhausting and painfully slow. Until the mid-1800s, farmers and farmhands spent seventy-five to ninety hours to plant and pick 2.5 acres of corn. This amount of land usually produced enough corn to fill one hundred bushels.

In the 1850s, new farm technology was invented. Bigger plows turned over the land. New machines dropped large amounts of seeds. These inventions used animal power. By the 1890s, when horses and mules hauled these machines through the fields, farm workers needed only thirty-five to forty hours to manage 2.5 acres. And they could still produce one hundred bushels of corn.

Women and girls who were part of the United States' farming communities also faced hardships in the 1800s. They often had to help in the fields during the busy planting and harvesting seasons. But they were also responsible for the household chores. Women and older girls wore ankle-length, long-sleeved dresses. Their clothing made them extremely uncomfortable as they worked in the fields under the hot summer sun.

Farming families faced many challenges, such as locust swarms, that could eat away their crops. It was important that everyone help out.

Mothers served as the moral counselors in the family. They taught their children how to behave. Daughters were encouraged to take part in homemaking activities such as cooking, washing clothes, and sewing.

On the other hand, sons were expected to be strong and protective of the family. They did most of the heavy, day-to-day field work.

Enslaved People on Plantations

Before the Civil War, large southern plantations were farmed by enslaved people. They normally planted huge cash crops, such as tobacco, cotton, and sugar cane. The plantations were basically small communities that served the needs of the owners' families. The main house, where the plantation owner lived, was often large with many rooms. The living quarters for enslaved people were typically simple one-room cabins with mud floors and, often, leaky roofs.

As many as a dozen enslaved people lived in each small cabin. They frequently hung a cloth from the ceiling to create a sense of privacy. A stone fireplace in the center of the floor provided the only heat. Simple holes were cut into the log walls to provide windows.

The plantation property usually held many other buildings, such as barns, work sheds, carriage houses, smokehouses, a cook's house, and a wash house. Some plantations even had a jail to imprison enslaved people who angered the owner.

Enslaved people had no rights. They were considered the property of the plantation owners. Enslaved people often worried that they would be sold and separated from their loved ones. Husbands were separated from wives. Mothers were separated from their children. Many brothers and sisters never got to know one another.

Children of enslaved people never attended school. When they were old enough, most of them would begin work in the fields.

11

Enslaved children never attended school. They usually started working in the fields by the age of seven or eight. Others were trained to be domestic workers and worked in the main house.

Domestic workers did all of the housekeeping for the plantation owner and his family. Their work included cooking, serving, cleaning, sewing, mending, washing, and the pressing of clothing.

There were some benefits to being a domestic worker. Most were given decent clothing to wear, so they looked presentable. They were fed better food, so they stayed healthy and did not make the owner's family sick. Sometimes, domestic workers even slept on the floor of the basement or attic of the main house.

Cotton boll

Workers in the fields did much more physical work. They were expected to start their jobs before dawn and often finished long after sunset. They even worked late into the night if the moonlight was bright and seasonal work had to be done.

If enslaved people tried to escape, they risked death. On some plantations, overseers hired men on horseback to patrol the fields with rifles and watch for runaways.

Many enslaved people picked crops such as cotton on plantations. They often lugged two large cotton sacks into the fields each morning. All day long they snapped cotton bolls off plants, with only a short break for lunch.

Some overseers hired men to watch the fields for runaways. Field workers began their day before the sun was up and worked until sundown, stopping only for lunch.

Once their two sacks were filled, the enslaved workers dragged them to the edge of the field. There the cotton was weighed and loaded onto wagons. Then they returned to the field to repeat this same tiring process.

Each person was expected to pick one hundred to two hundred pounds of cotton each day. If they didn't pick enough, they could be whipped. Enslaved people worked in the heat and in the rain. It was their job to plant and harvest the crops as quickly as possible.

Enslaved people also had other chores on the plantation that kept them busy late into the night. They cared for the livestock and chopped wood for themselves and the people living in the main house. They also had to find time to prepare their own meals and mend their clothing.

This etching shows a family of enslaved workers enjoying a rare moment of free time.

Between working the fields and their daily chores, enslaved people were left with little time for pleasure. But many enslaved people expressed their **identities** and strong feelings through music. They composed sad songs, and this powerful music became the basis for a type of music known as the blues. Work songs were sung while in the fields each day. They even composed gospel music that they sang when they prayed together. Much of this music is an important part of American culture today.

Sharecroppers

Sharecropping developed in the South and the Midwest after the Civil War ended in 1865. Most sharecroppers were either formerly enslaved people or poor white people.

Sharecroppers couldn't afford to buy land, so they **leased** it. They also leased most of the supplies they needed to farm the land. Many sharecroppers had to buy food on credit to feed their families until they made money from their harvests.

The terms of the leases were often unfair. Many landowners took advantage of their tenants, since few sharecroppers could read or write. Sharecroppers also paid very high prices for food and supplies they bought on credit.

Since many sharecroppers promised the landowner fifty percent of their crops, they were desperate to produce successful ones. The entire family pitched in to work the leased land. They needed to get the best possible prices at the market in order to repay the landowner. Unfortunately, sharecroppers rarely made enough money from their harvests to do this.

Sharecropping was especially hard on women and children. They helped in the fields during the planting and harvesting seasons. They also took care of the family garden, which provided much of the food they ate.

Women and children were also responsible for the household chores. They cooked, cleaned, sewed, mended, and hauled water. They made candles, soap, and other objects for the home. There was rarely enough food available for second helpings or leftovers.

Children of sharecroppers worked in the fields with their parents in order to bring in a successful crop.

The children of sharecroppers often did not attend school. The typical one-room school was often miles from the farm. The daily walk was difficult and time-consuming. Many children didn't even own shoes to make the journey.

Southern rural schools tended to have winter and summer terms. But many older children, especially boys, couldn't attend school in the summer. They had to help their parents in the fields.

Many girls didn't go to school at all. They had to help their mothers do household chores. They helped cook meals and wash the family's clothes.

Families worked together in the field and in the house to keep the farm running. In order to help their parents, children often did not attend school.

Washing clothes was hard work. First, the girls soaked the clothing in large pots of boiling water and soap. Then, they pounded out the soap suds and remaining dirt with a battling stick, which looked like a wooden paddle.

Parents hoped that schooling would make a better life for their children possible. But this usually became an impossible dream. Every family member was needed in order to keep the farm running.

Apple Orchards

Apple orchards today are often full of neat rows of apple trees. But the creation of a successful orchard in the 1800s required the cooperation of all the laborers—either family members or hired hands—and other forces.

Bad weather, insects, or diseases could ruin an entire crop of apples. Even a surplus could be troublesome. Too many apples meant the market prices dropped and the orchard owner's profit dropped as well.

Very little work in the orchard was done by machines. When it was time to pick the apples, each apple had to be removed by hand so the fruit and the tree's branches were not damaged. Every apple tree was valuable and expected to provide years of fruit.

The family home on an apple orchard was generally more comfortable and spacious than the small homes of sharecroppers and enslaved people. But life on the orchard was still difficult.

Orchard owners often had new kitchen tools, such as stoves. The kitchen stove replaced the fireplace, used by enslaved people and sharecroppers for cooking. However, the stove had to be fed with wood, which needed to be chopped and stored. Women and girls in long, uncomfortable dresses had to handle these new tasks.

In the end, devices such as stoves increased the number of daily chores that were the responsibility of women and girls. The new equipment improved the family's living standards, but it also increased the workload.

Running an apple orchard, such as this one in Colorado, was hard work for the family and hired hands who tended it.

Most children who grew up on orchards had better lives than enslaved children or the children of sharecroppers. Children who lived on orchards had better clothing, food, and a chance to go to school. During some months of the year, the children had some free time from their chores in the orchard. They could make the long walk to and from their one-room school house.

Classes at a typical school went up to the eighth grade. The students studied different levels of reading, writing, arithmetic, and history. Notebooks and paper were rarely used since paper was very expensive. Instead, children wrote on slate boards, which looked like small, hand-held chalkboards. These chalkboards could be erased easily and reused. However, most learning was done by memorization. Students repeated words or lessons until they had committed them to memory.

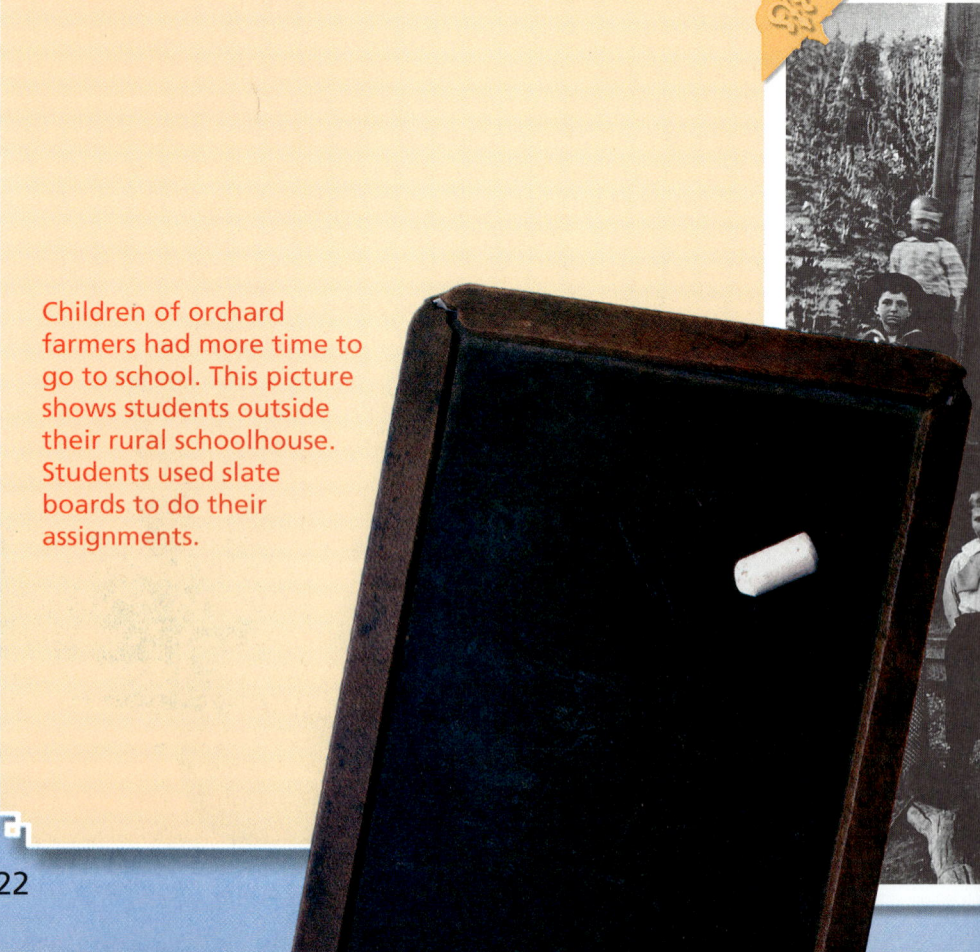

Children of orchard farmers had more time to go to school. This picture shows students outside their rural schoolhouse. Students used slate boards to do their assignments.

Life in the 1800s

Throughout the United States in the 1800s, the people who worked the land completed long lists of chores every single day. All these Americans, from enslaved people and sharecroppers to the owners of orchards, learned to rely on their own skills and abilities to make the best of their situations. To give up meant failure—personal failure and failure for the people who depended on them. Life was challenging for all the people who farmed land. But everyone worked hard and dreamed of one day reaching a brighter future.

Glossary

counselors *n.* people who give advice.

identities *n.* qualities of being who or what you are; individualities.

kerosene *n.* a thin oil distilled from petroleum; coal oil.

leased *v.* rented.

physical *adj.* of or for the body.

surplus *n.* an amount over and above what is needed.

technology *n.* the use of scientific knowledge to control physical objects and forces.